SLOW COOKER DOG FOOD COOKBOOK FOR BEAGLE

Dr. Wesley Glasgow

TABLE OF CONTENTS

INTRODUCTION

In the tapestry of my life, there exists a thread woven with love, devotion, and a steadfast bond with man's best friend. It all began with a fuzzy, wriggling bundle of joy named Dan. From the moment my parents placed him in my arms, his warm, trusting gaze captured my heart, and I knew that my destiny was forever entwined with his.

As a lifelong dog lover, my childhood dreams were filled with visions of endless adventures with my furry companion. Dan wasn't just a pet; he was my confidant, my playmate, and my constant source of joy. Together, we explored the world with boundless enthusiasm, leaving a trail of paw prints etched upon the canvas of my memories.

But amidst the laughter and the tail-wagging joy, there lurked a shadow – a darkness that threatened to eclipse our idyllic bond. You see, in my youthful exuberance and boundless affection, I made a grave mistake that would forever alter the course of our lives.

I lavished Dan with all the treats and indulgences his heart desired, believing that my love could sustain him through anything. Little did I know, my well-intentioned gestures were leading him down a treacherous path of poor health and suffering.

As the years passed, I watched in anguish as Dan's once-vibrant spirit began to dim. His playful antics gave way to lethargy, his glossy coat lost its luster, and his once-bright eyes clouded with pain. It wasn't until he began to struggle with his weight and succumb to frequent bouts of illness that I realized the gravity of the situation.

The turning point came when Dan was diagnosed with diabetes – a diagnosis that struck like a thunderbolt, shattering the illusion of invincibility that I had so naively clung to. My beloved companion, my faithful friend, was suffering, and I was powerless to ease his pain.

As I stood by Dan's side in the sterile confines of the veterinarian's office, a fire ignited within me – a burning resolve to right the wrongs I had unwittingly inflicted upon him. I vowed to embark on a journey of discovery, to unlock the secrets of canine nutrition and heal Dan from the inside out.

And so, my quest began – a journey fuelled by love, driven by determination, and guided by a steadfast commitment to my loyal companion. I immersed myself in the study of canine nutrition, devouring every book, attending every seminar, and consulting every expert in search of answers.

Through trial and error, sweat and tears, I discovered the transformative power of good nutrition. I witnessed firsthand the miraculous changes that occurred when I swapped out Dan's processed kibble for homemade meals crafted with love and care. His coat regained its sheen, his energy soared, and his spirit blossomed with newfound vitality.

From that moment on, I dedicated my life to finding the best recipes for dogs – recipes that nourished not just their bodies, but their souls as well. And now, after 25 years of tireless dedication and unwavering devotion, I stand before you as Dr. Wesley Glasgow – veterinarian, chef, and advocate for the health and happiness of our canine companions.

In my journey to nourish the bodies and souls of dogs everywhere, I have tested and approved every recipe in this cookbook. I have shared them with my family, my friends, and my patients, all of whom have seen the positive impact of wholesome nutrition on their beloved Beagles.

This cookbook is more than just a collection of recipes; it is a celebration of the profound bond between humans and dogs. It is a testament to the power of love, the importance of nutrition, and the joy of sharing a meal with our furry friends. And above all, it is a promise – a promise to provide Beagle parents with the tools they need to nourish their companions and ensure a lifetime of health, happiness, and pawsitive vibes.

So join me as we embark on a culinary journey tailored specifically for Beagles. Let's explore the benefits of healthy eating, uncover the dangers of poor nutrition, and discover the countless advantages of embracing the recipes within these pages. Together, let's nourish our Beagles from the inside out and create a legacy of love that will last a lifetime.

Contact the Author

Thank you for reading my book! I would love to hear from you, whether you have feedback, questions, or just want to share your thoughts. Your feedback means a lot to me and helps me improve as a writer.

Please don't hesitate to reach out to me through

glasgowesley@gmail.com

I look forward to connecting with my readers and appreciate your support in this literary journey. Your thoughts and comments are valuable to me.

CHAPTER 1
Understanding Beagle Nutritional Needs

Beagles, beloved for their friendly demeanor and boundless energy, require a well-balanced diet to maintain their health and vitality. Just like any other breed, Beagles have specific nutritional needs that must be met to ensure they lead happy and healthy lives.

Beagle Dietary Requirements

Beagles are typically medium-sized dogs with a moderate activity level. As such, their dietary requirements may vary depending on factors such as age, weight, activity level, and overall health. However, there are some general guidelines to keep in mind when feeding a Beagle:

1. Protein: Beagles need a diet rich in high-quality protein to support their muscle development and overall health. Look for protein sources like lean meats (chicken, turkey, beef), fish, and eggs.

2. Fat: Fat is a concentrated source of energy for Beagles and is essential for maintaining healthy skin and coat. Opt for healthy sources of fat such as fish oil, flaxseed oil, and chicken fat.

3. Carbohydrates: Carbohydrates provide Beagles with the energy they need to stay active throughout the day. Choose complex carbohydrates like whole grains (brown rice, oats) and vegetables (sweet potatoes, peas) over simple carbohydrates.

4. Vitamins and minerals: Beagles require a balanced mix of vitamins and minerals to support various bodily functions, including bone health, immune function, and digestion. Ensure their diet includes a variety of fruits and vegetables to provide essential vitamins and minerals.

5. Water: Adequate hydration is crucial for Beagles to maintain their overall health and prevent dehydration. Always provide fresh, clean water for your Beagle to drink throughout the day.

Importance of Balanced Nutrition

Providing your Beagle with a balanced diet is essential for their overall health and well-being. A balanced diet helps prevent nutritional deficiencies and promotes proper growth and development. Additionally, a well-balanced diet can help prevent common health issues such as obesity, dental problems, and digestive issues.

Common Nutritional Issues in Beagles

Despite their seemingly robust appetites, Beagles are prone to certain nutritional issues that owners should be aware of:

1. Obesity: Beagles have a tendency to overeat if not monitored closely, which can lead to obesity and associated health problems such as joint issues and diabetes. It's important to feed Beagles appropriate portion sizes and provide regular exercise to help them maintain a healthy weight.

2. Food allergies: Some Beagles may develop food allergies or sensitivities to certain ingredients in their diet. Common allergens include grains, beef, dairy, and chicken. If you suspect your Beagle has a food allergy, consult with your veterinarian to determine the best course of action.

3. Dental problems: Beagles are prone to dental issues such as plaque buildup and gum disease, which can be exacerbated by poor diet choices. Feeding your Beagle a diet rich in dental-friendly foods, such as raw bones or dental chews, can help promote good oral health.

CHAPTER 2
Benefits of Slow Cooker Dog Food

Slow cooker dog food offers several advantages over traditional methods of feeding your furry friend. By taking advantage of the slow cooking process, you can provide your dog with nutritious, homemade meals that promote their health and well-being.

Advantages of Homemade Meals

1. Control over ingredients: When preparing homemade meals in a slow cooker for your dog, you have full control over the quality and source of ingredients. This allows you to tailor your dog's diet to their specific dietary needs and preferences, ensuring they receive optimal nutrition.

2. Avoidance of fillers and additives: Many commercial dog foods contain fillers, additives, and preservatives that may not be beneficial for your dog's health. By making homemade meals, you can eliminate these unnecessary ingredients and provide your dog with wholesome, natural foods.

3. Customization for dietary restrictions: If your dog has food allergies, sensitivities, or specific dietary restrictions, homemade meals allow you to carefully select ingredients that won't trigger adverse reactions. This customization can help alleviate digestive issues and promote better overall health.

Slow Cooking for Optimal Nutrition

1. Retention of nutrients: Slow cooking allows ingredients to simmer and meld together, resulting in a flavorful and nutrient-rich meal for your dog. Unlike

high-heat cooking methods that can degrade nutrients, slow cooking helps preserve the integrity of vitamins, minerals, and other essential nutrients.

2. Enhanced digestibility: The gentle cooking process of a slow cooker breaks down tough fibers in meats and vegetables, making them easier for your dog to digest. This can be especially beneficial for dogs with sensitive stomachs or digestive issues.

3. Release of natural flavors: Slow cooking allows ingredients to release their natural flavors and aromas, enticing even the pickiest of eaters. The resulting meal is not only nutritious but also delicious, encouraging your dog to enjoy their food and eat with enthusiasm.

Cost-Effectiveness and Convenience

1. Economical: Making dog food in a slow cooker can be a cost-effective alternative to purchasing commercial dog food, especially if you buy ingredients in bulk or take advantage of seasonal produce. Plus, you can use affordable cuts of meat and incorporate leftover vegetables to minimize waste.

2. Batch cooking: Slow cookers are ideal for batch cooking, allowing you to prepare large quantities of dog food at once and freeze individual portions for later use. This saves time and effort in meal preparation while ensuring your dog always has a supply of fresh, homemade meals on hand.

3. Timesaving: Once ingredients are prepped and added to the slow cooker, minimal supervision is required, freeing up time for other tasks or activities. You can set it and forget it, returning hours later to a delicious and nutritious meal ready to serve to your furry companion.

CHAPTER 3
Essential Ingredients for Beagle Health

To ensure the optimal health and well-being of your Beagle, it's important to include specific essential ingredients in their diet. These ingredients provide essential nutrients that support various bodily functions and promote overall health.

Quality Proteins:

Proteins are the building blocks of your Beagle's body and are essential for muscle development, tissue repair, and overall growth. When selecting protein sources for your Beagle, opt for high-quality, lean proteins such as:

- Chicken

- Turkey

- Beef

- Fish

- Eggs

These protein sources provide essential amino acids that are necessary for your Beagle's health and vitality.

Nutrient-Rich Vegetables:

Vegetables are an excellent source of essential vitamins, minerals, and antioxidants that support your Beagle's immune system, digestion, and overall health. Incorporate a variety of nutrient-rich vegetables into your Beagle's diet, such as:

- Sweet potatoes

- Carrots

- Green beans

- Peas

- Spinach

These vegetables provide essential nutrients like vitamin A, vitamin C, fiber, and phytonutrients, which are beneficial for your Beagle's health.

Healthy Fats and Oils:

Healthy fats and oils are essential for your Beagle's skin health, coat condition, and overall well-being. Incorporate sources of healthy fats and oils into your Beagle's diet, such as:

- Fish oil

- Flaxseed oil

- Coconut oil

- Olive oil

These fats provide essential fatty acids, such as omega-3 and omega-6, which support your Beagle's cardiovascular health, brain function, and inflammatory response.

Supplements for Beagle Wellness:

In addition to a balanced diet, certain supplements can support your Beagle's overall wellness and address specific health concerns. Consider incorporating the following supplements into your Beagle's routine:

- Glucosamine and chondroitin: These supplements support joint health and mobility, which is particularly important for aging Beagles or those prone to joint issues.

- Probiotics: Probiotic supplements promote a healthy balance of gut bacteria, which can support digestion and immune function.

- Omega-3 fatty acids: Omega-3 supplements can support skin health, coat condition, and reduce inflammation in Beagles with skin allergies or joint issues.

Before introducing any supplements into your Beagle's diet, consult with your veterinarian to ensure they are appropriate and safe for your dog's individual needs.

By incorporating these essential ingredients into your Beagle's diet, you can provide them with the nutrients they need to thrive and lead a happy, healthy life.

OTHER BOOKS BY THE AUTHOR

INSTANT POT DOG FOOD COOKBOOK

DOG FOOD COOKBOOK FOR PICKY EATERS

AIR FRYER DOG FOOD COOKBOOK

SLOW COOKER DOG FOOD COOKBOOK

DOG FOOD COOKBOOK FOR SENSITIVE STOMACH

SCAN THE QR CODE TO SEE MORE BOOKS BY AUTHOR

CHAPTER 4

Breakfast and Brunch Ideas

Turkey and Egg Casserole

Servings: 6 Cooking Time: 4 hours on low

Ingredients:

- 1 lb ground turkey
- 6 eggs
- 1 cup diced sweet potatoes
- 1 cup chopped spinach
- 1 cup grated carrots
- 1 cup low-sodium chicken broth

Instructions:

1. In a skillet, cook ground turkey until browned. Drain excess fat.
2. In a bowl, beat the eggs.
3. In the slow cooker, layer cooked ground turkey, diced sweet potatoes, chopped spinach, and grated carrots.
4. Pour beaten eggs and low-sodium chicken broth over the ingredients.
5. Cover and cook on low for 4 hours or until eggs are set.
6. Allow to cool before serving.

Nutritional Information: Protein: 22g, Fat: 10g, Carbohydrates: 16g, Fiber: 4g

Chicken and Quinoa Breakfast Bowl

Servings: 4 Cooking Time: 3 hours on low

Ingredients:

- 2 boneless, skinless chicken breasts

- 1 cup cooked quinoa

- 1 cup diced apples

- 1 cup chopped broccoli

- 1 cup low-sodium chicken broth

Instructions:

1. Place chicken breasts in the slow cooker.

2. Add cooked quinoa, diced apples, and chopped broccoli on top of the chicken.

3. Pour low-sodium chicken broth over the ingredients.

4. Cover and cook on low for 3 hours or until chicken is cooked through.

5. Shred the chicken using forks before serving.

6. Allow to cool before serving.

Nutritional Information: Protein: 24g, Fat: 4g, Carbohydrates: 20g, Fiber: 5g

Beef and Potato Hash

Servings: 4 Cooking Time: 4 hours on low

Ingredients:

- 1 lb lean beef stew meat, diced

- 2 cups diced potatoes

- 1 cup diced bell peppers

- 1 cup chopped green beans

- 1 cup low-sodium beef broth

Instructions:

1. In the slow cooker, combine diced beef stew meat, diced potatoes, diced bell peppers, and chopped green beans.

2. Pour low-sodium beef broth over the ingredients.

3. Cover and cook on low for 4 hours or until beef is tender and vegetables are cooked through.

4. Allow to cool before serving.

Nutritional Information: Protein: 24g, Fat: 10g, Carbohydrates: 18g, Fiber: 4g

Salmon and Sweet Potato Frittata

Servings: 6 Cooking Time: 3 hours on low

Ingredients:

- 1 can (14 oz) salmon, drained and flaked

- 4 eggs

- 1 cup diced sweet potatoes

- 1 cup chopped spinach

- 1 cup low-sodium vegetable broth

Instructions:

1. In a bowl, beat the eggs.

2. In the slow cooker, layer flaked salmon, diced sweet potatoes, and chopped spinach.

3. Pour beaten eggs and low-sodium vegetable broth over the ingredients.

4. Cover and cook on low for 3 hours or until eggs are set.

5. Allow to cool before serving.

Nutritional Information: Protein: 20g, Fat: 8g, Carbohydrates: 16g, Fiber: 3g

Chicken and Brown Rice Porridge

Servings: 4 Cooking Time: 4 hours on low

Ingredients:

- 2 boneless, skinless chicken breasts

- 1 cup brown rice

- 2 cups low-sodium chicken broth

- 1 cup diced carrots

- 1 cup chopped kale

Instructions:

1. Place chicken breasts in the slow cooker.

2. Add brown rice, low-sodium chicken broth, diced carrots, and chopped kale on top of the chicken.

3. Cover and cook on low for 4 hours or until chicken is cooked through and rice is tender.

4. Shred the chicken using forks before serving.

5. Allow to cool before serving.

Nutritional Information: Protein: 20g, Fat: 4g, Carbohydrates: 24g, Fiber: 5g

Turkey and Cranberry Breakfast Bake

Servings: 6 Cooking Time: 3 hours on low

Ingredients:

- 1 lb ground turkey

- 1 cup rolled oats

- 1/2 cup dried cranberries, chopped

- 1 cup grated carrots

- 1 cup low-sodium chicken broth

Instructions:

1. In a skillet, cook ground turkey until browned. Drain excess fat.

2. In the slow cooker, layer cooked ground turkey, rolled oats, chopped dried cranberries, and grated carrots.

3. Pour low-sodium chicken broth over the ingredients.

4. Cover and cook on low for 3 hours or until oats are cooked through.

5. Allow to cool before serving.

Nutritional Information: Protein: 18g, Fat: 6g, Carbohydrates: 16g, Fiber: 3g

Beef and Veggie Breakfast Stew

Servings: 4 Cooking Time: 4 hours on low

Ingredients:

- 1 lb lean beef stew meat, cubed

- 2 cups diced potatoes

- 1 cup diced zucchini

- 1 cup chopped green beans

- 1 cup low-sodium beef broth

Instructions:

1. In the slow cooker, combine diced beef stew meat, diced potatoes, diced zucchini, and chopped green beans.

2. Pour low-sodium beef broth over the ingredients.

3. Cover and cook on low for 4 hours or until beef is tender and vegetables are cooked through.

4. Allow to cool before serving.

Nutritional Information: Protein: 24g, Fat: 10g, Carbohydrates: 20g, Fiber: 4g

Chicken and Pumpkin Oatmeal

Servings: 4 Cooking Time: 3 hours on low

Ingredients:

- 2 boneless, skinless chicken breasts

- 1 cup rolled oats

- 1 cup pumpkin puree

- 2 cups low-sodium chicken broth

- 1 teaspoon ground cinnamon

Instructions:

1. Place chicken breasts in the slow cooker.

2. Add rolled oats, pumpkin puree, low-sodium chicken broth, and ground cinnamon on top of the chicken.

3. Cover and cook on low for 3 hours or until chicken is cooked through and oats are tender.

4. Shred the chicken using forks before serving.

5. Allow to cool before serving.

Nutritional Information: Protein: 20g, Fat: 4g, Carbohydrates: 24g, Fiber: 5g

Salmon and Spinach Omelette

Servings: 4 Cooking Time: 3 hours on low

Ingredients:

- 1 can (14 oz) salmon, drained and flaked

- 6 eggs

- 1 cup chopped spinach

- 1 cup diced tomatoes

- 1 cup low-sodium vegetable broth

Instructions:

1. In a bowl, beat the eggs.

2. In the slow cooker, layer flaked salmon, chopped spinach, and diced tomatoes.

3. Pour beaten eggs and low-sodium vegetable broth over the ingredients.

4. Cover and cook on low for 3 hours or until eggs are set.

5. Allow to cool before serving.

Nutritional Information: Protein: 20g, Fat: 8g, Carbohydrates: 16g, Fiber: 3g

Beef and Barley Breakfast Stew

Servings: 4 Cooking Time: 4 hours on low

Ingredients:

- 1 lb lean beef stew meat, cubed

- 1 cup pearl barley

- 1 cup diced carrots

- 1 cup chopped celery

- 1 cup low-sodium beef broth

Instructions:

1. In the slow cooker, combine diced beef stew meat, pearl barley, diced carrots, and chopped celery.

2. Pour low-sodium beef broth over the ingredients.

3. Cover and cook on low for 4 hours or until beef is tender and barley is cooked through.

4. Allow to cool before serving.

Nutritional Information: Protein: 24g, Fat: 10g, Carbohydrates: 20g, Fiber: 4g

CHAPTER 5

Nourishing Soups and Stews

Chicken and Rice Soup

Servings: 6 Cooking Time: 4 hours on low

Ingredients:

- 2 boneless, skinless chicken breasts
- 1 cup brown rice
- 2 cups chopped carrots
- 2 cups chopped spinach
- 4 cups low-sodium chicken broth

Instructions:

1. Place chicken breasts in the slow cooker.

2. Add brown rice, chopped carrots, and chopped spinach on top of the chicken.

3. Pour low-sodium chicken broth over the ingredients.

4. Cover and cook on low for 4 hours or until chicken is cooked through and rice is tender.

5. Shred the chicken using forks before serving.

6. Allow to cool before serving.

Nutritional Information: Protein: 22g, Fat: 4g, Carbohydrates: 24g, Fiber: 5g

Beef and Barley Stew

Servings: 6 Cooking Time: 6 hours on low

Ingredients:

- 1 lb lean beef stew meat, cubed

- 1 cup pearl barley

- 2 cups chopped potatoes

- 2 cups chopped green beans

- 4 cups low-sodium beef broth

Instructions:

1. In the slow cooker, combine cubed beef stew meat, pearl barley, chopped potatoes, and chopped green beans.

2. Pour low-sodium beef broth over the ingredients.

3. Cover and cook on low for 6 hours or until beef is tender and barley is cooked through.

4. Allow to cool before serving.

Nutritional Information: Protein: 24g, Fat: 10g, Carbohydrates: 28g, Fiber: 6g

Turkey and Vegetable Soup

Servings: 6 Cooking Time: 4 hours on low

Ingredients:

- 1 lb ground turkey

- 2 cups chopped broccoli

- 1 cup diced potatoes

- 1 cup chopped bell peppers

- 4 cups low-sodium vegetable broth

Instructions:

1. In a skillet, cook ground turkey until browned. Drain excess fat.

2. Place cooked ground turkey in the slow cooker.

3. Add chopped broccoli, diced potatoes, and chopped bell peppers to the slow cooker.

4. Pour low-sodium vegetable broth over the ingredients.

5. Cover and cook on low for 4 hours.

6. Stir well before serving.

Nutritional Information: Protein: 22g, Fat: 8g, Carbohydrates: 18g, Fiber: 5g

Salmon and Potato Chowder

Servings: 4 Cooking Time: 3 hours on low

Ingredients:

- 2 cans (14 oz each) salmon, drained and flaked

- 2 cups diced potatoes

- 1 cup chopped broccoli

- 1 cup chopped carrots

- 4 cups low-sodium vegetable broth

Instructions:

1. Place flaked salmon, diced potatoes, chopped broccoli, and chopped carrots in the slow cooker.

2. Pour low-sodium vegetable broth over the ingredients.

3. Cover and cook on low for 3 hours.

4. Stir well before serving.

Nutritional Information: Protein: 20g, Fat: 10g, Carbohydrates: 22g, Fiber: 5g

Chicken and Lentil Stew

Servings: 4 Cooking Time: 4 hours on low

Ingredients:

- 2 boneless, skinless chicken breasts

- 1 cup dry lentils, rinsed

- 2 cups chopped spinach

- 1 cup diced sweet potatoes

- 4 cups low-sodium chicken broth

Instructions:

1. Place chicken breasts in the slow cooker.

2. Add dry lentils, chopped spinach, and diced sweet potatoes on top of the chicken.

3. Pour low-sodium chicken broth over the ingredients.

4. Cover and cook on low for 4 hours.

5. Shred the chicken using forks before serving.

Nutritional Information: Protein: 20g, Fat: 4g, Carbohydrates: 24g, Fiber: 6g

Turkey and Lentil Soup

Servings: 6 Cooking Time: 4 hours on low

Ingredients:

- 1 lb ground turkey

- 1 cup dry lentils, rinsed

- 2 cups chopped kale

- 1 cup diced tomatoes

- 4 cups low-sodium vegetable broth

Instructions:

1. In a skillet, cook ground turkey until browned. Drain excess fat.

2. Place cooked ground turkey in the slow cooker.

3. Add dry lentils, chopped kale, and diced tomatoes to the slow cooker.

4. Pour low-sodium vegetable broth over the ingredients.

5. Cover and cook on low for 4 hours.

6. Stir well before serving.

Nutritional Information: Protein: 22g, Fat: 8g, Carbohydrates: 18g, Fiber: 5g

Beef and Pumpkin Stew

Servings: 4 Cooking Time: 6 hours on low

Ingredients:

- 1 lb lean beef stew meat, cubed

- 2 cups diced pumpkin

- 1 cup chopped kale

- 1 cup diced carrots

- 4 cups low-sodium beef broth

Instructions:

1. Place cubed beef stew meat in the slow cooker.

2. Add diced pumpkin, chopped kale, and diced carrots on top of the beef.

3. Pour low-sodium beef broth over the ingredients.

4. Cover and cook on low for 6 hours.

5. Stir well before serving.

Nutritional Information: Protein: 24g, Fat: 10g, Carbohydrates: 20g, Fiber: 5g

Chicken and Vegetable Stew

Servings: 6 Cooking Time: 4 hours on low

Ingredients:

- 2 boneless, skinless chicken breasts

- 2 cups chopped carrots

- 1 cup chopped celery

- 1 cup diced potatoes

- 4 cups low-sodium chicken broth

Instructions:

1. Place chicken breasts in the slow cooker.

2. Add chopped carrots, chopped celery, and diced potatoes on top of the chicken.

3. Pour low-sodium chicken broth over the ingredients.

4. Cover and cook on low for 4 hours.

5. Shred the chicken using forks before serving.

Nutritional Information: Protein: 22g, Fat: 4g, Carbohydrates: 20g, Fiber: 4g

Turkey and Veggie Stew

Servings: 6 Cooking Time: 4 hours on low

Ingredients:

- 1 lb ground turkey

- 2 cups chopped zucchini

- 1 cup chopped green beans

- 1 cup diced tomatoes

- 4 cups low-sodium vegetable broth

Instructions:

1. In a skillet, cook ground turkey until browned. Drain excess fat.

2. Place cooked ground turkey in the slow cooker.

3. Add chopped zucchini, chopped green beans, and diced tomatoes to the slow cooker.

4. Pour low-sodium vegetable broth over the ingredients.

5. Cover and cook on low for 4 hours.

6. Stir well before serving.

Nutritional Information: Protein: 22g, Fat: 8g, Carbohydrates: 18g, Fiber: 5g

Beef and Vegetable Soup

Servings: 6 Cooking Time: 4 hours on low

Ingredients:

- 1 lb lean beef stew meat, cubed

- 2 cups chopped broccoli

- 1 cup diced potatoes

- 1 cup chopped bell peppers

- 4 cups low-sodium beef broth

Instructions:

1. In the slow cooker, combine cubed beef stew meat, chopped broccoli, diced potatoes, and chopped bell peppers.

2. Pour low-sodium beef broth over the ingredients.

3. Cover and cook on low for 4 hours.

4. Stir well before serving.

Nutritional Information: Protein: 24g, Fat: 10g, Carbohydrates: 20g, Fiber: 4g

CHAPTER 6
Wholesome Main Courses

Turkey and Sweet Potato Stew

Servings: 4 Cooking Time: 4 hours on low

Ingredients:

- 1 lb ground turkey

- 2 cups diced sweet potatoes

- 1 cup chopped carrots

- 1 cup green peas

- 4 cups low-sodium turkey or chicken broth

Instructions:

1. In a skillet, cook ground turkey until browned. Drain excess fat.

2. Place cooked ground turkey in the slow cooker.

3. Add diced sweet potatoes, chopped carrots, and green peas to the slow cooker.

4. Pour low-sodium turkey or chicken broth over the ingredients.

5. Cover and cook on low for 4 hours.

6. Stir well before serving.

Nutritional Information: Protein: 22g, Fat: 8g, Carbohydrates: 20g, Fiber: 5g

Beef and Vegetable Stew

Servings: 4 Cooking Time: 6 hours on low

Ingredients:

- 1 lb lean beef stew meat, cubed

- 2 cups diced potatoes

- 1 cup chopped celery

- 1 cup chopped carrots

- 4 cups low-sodium beef broth

Instructions:

1. In the slow cooker, combine cubed beef stew meat, diced potatoes, chopped celery, and chopped carrots.

2. Pour low-sodium beef broth over the ingredients.

3. Cover and cook on low for 6 hours or until beef is tender and vegetables are cooked through.

4. Stir well before serving.

Nutritional Information: Protein: 24g, Fat: 10g, Carbohydrates: 20g, Fiber: 4g

Chicken and Rice Casserole

Servings: 4 Cooking Time: 4 hours on low

Ingredients:

- 2 boneless, skinless chicken breasts
- 1 cup brown rice
- 2 cups chopped broccoli
- 1 cup chopped carrots
- 4 cups low-sodium chicken broth

Instructions:

1. Place chicken breasts in the slow cooker.
2. Add brown rice, chopped broccoli, and chopped carrots on top of the chicken.
3. Pour low-sodium chicken broth over the ingredients.
4. Cover and cook on low for 4 hours or until chicken is cooked through and rice is tender.
5. Shred the chicken using forks before serving.
6. Stir well before serving.

Nutritional Information: Protein: 22g, Fat: 4g, Carbohydrates: 24g, Fiber: 5g

Salmon and Vegetable Medley

Servings: 4 Cooking Time: 3 hours on low

Ingredients:

- 2 cans (14 oz each) salmon, drained and flaked

- 2 cups chopped zucchini

- 1 cup chopped bell peppers

- 1 cup diced tomatoes

- 4 cups low-sodium vegetable broth

Instructions:

1. In the slow cooker, combine flaked salmon, chopped zucchini, chopped bell peppers, and diced tomatoes.

2. Pour low-sodium vegetable broth over the ingredients.

3. Cover and cook on low for 3 hours.

4. Stir well before serving.

Nutritional Information: Protein: 20g, Fat: 10g, Carbohydrates: 22g, Fiber: 5g

Turkey and Quinoa Pilaf

Servings: 4 Cooking Time: 3 hours on low

Ingredients:

- 1 lb ground turkey

- 1 cup cooked quinoa

- 2 cups chopped spinach

- 1 cup diced sweet potatoes

- 4 cups low-sodium turkey or chicken broth

Instructions:

1. In a skillet, cook ground turkey until browned. Drain excess fat.

2. Place cooked ground turkey in the slow cooker.

3. Add cooked quinoa, chopped spinach, and diced sweet potatoes to the slow cooker.

4. Pour low-sodium turkey or chicken broth over the ingredients.

5. Cover and cook on low for 3 hours.

6. Stir well before serving.

Nutritional Information: Protein: 22g, Fat: 8g, Carbohydrates: 20g, Fiber: 5g

Beef and Barley Risotto

Servings: 4 Cooking Time: 6 hours on low

Ingredients:

- 1 lb lean beef stew meat, cubed

- 1 cup pearl barley

- 2 cups chopped mushrooms

- 1 cup diced onions

- 4 cups low-sodium beef broth

Instructions:

1. In the slow cooker, combine cubed beef stew meat, pearl barley, chopped mushrooms, and diced onions.

2. Pour low-sodium beef broth over the ingredients.

3. Cover and cook on low for 6 hours or until beef is tender and barley is cooked through.

4. Stir well before serving.

Nutritional Information: Protein: 24g, Fat: 10g, Carbohydrates: 28g, Fiber: 6g

Chicken and Lentil Curry

Servings: 4 Cooking Time: 4 hours on low

Ingredients:

- 2 boneless, skinless chicken breasts

- 1 cup dry lentils, rinsed

- 2 cups chopped tomatoes

- 1 cup chopped bell peppers

- 4 cups low-sodium chicken broth

Instructions:

1. Place chicken breasts in the slow cooker.

2. Add dry lentils, chopped tomatoes, and chopped bell peppers to the slow cooker.

3. Pour low-sodium chicken broth over the ingredients.

4. Cover and cook on low for 4 hours.

5. Shred the chicken using forks before serving.

6. Stir well before serving.

Nutritional Information: Protein: 20g, Fat: 4g, Carbohydrates: 24g, Fiber: 6g

Turkey and Vegetable Stir-Fry

Servings: 4 Cooking Time: 3 hours on low

Ingredients:

- 1 lb ground turkey

- 2 cups chopped broccoli

- 1 cup sliced carrots

- 1 cup chopped bell peppers

- 4 cups low-sodium vegetable broth

Instructions:

1. In a skillet, cook ground turkey until browned. Drain excess fat.

2. Place cooked ground turkey in the slow cooker.

3. Add chopped broccoli, sliced carrots, and chopped bell peppers to the slow cooker.

4. Pour low-sodium vegetable broth over the ingredients.

5. Cover and cook on low for 3 hours.

6. Stir well before serving.

Nutritional Information: Protein: 22g, Fat: 8g, Carbohydrates: 18g, Fiber: 5g

Beef and Potato Curry

Servings: 4 Cooking Time: 6 hours on low

Ingredients:

- 1 lb lean beef stew meat, cubed

- 2 cups diced potatoes

- 1 cup chopped onions

- 1 cup chopped tomatoes

- 4 cups low-sodium beef broth

Instructions:

1. In the slow cooker, combine cubed beef stew meat, diced potatoes, chopped onions, and chopped tomatoes.

2. Pour low-sodium beef broth over the ingredients.

3. Cover and cook on low for 6 hours or until beef is tender and potatoes are cooked through.

4. Stir well before serving.

Nutritional Information: Protein: 24g, Fat: 10g, Carbohydrates: 20g, Fiber: 4g

Salmon and Spinach Risotto

Servings: 4 Cooking Time: 4 hours on low

Ingredients:

- 2 cans (14 oz each) salmon, drained and flaked

- 1 cup arborio rice

- 2 cups chopped spinach

- 1 cup diced tomatoes

- 4 cups low-sodium vegetable broth

Instructions:

1. In the slow cooker, combine flaked salmon, arborio rice, chopped spinach, and diced tomatoes.

2. Pour low-sodium vegetable broth over the ingredients.

3. Cover and cook on low for 4 hours.

4. Stir well before serving.

Nutritional Information: Protein: 20g, Fat: 10g, Carbohydrates: 22g, Fiber: 5g

<h1 style="text-align:center">CHAPTER 7</h1>

<h1 style="text-align:center">Delicious Treats and Snacks</h1>

Peanut Butter and Banana Biscuits

Servings: Varies Cooking Time: 3 hours on low

Ingredients:

- 1 cup mashed ripe bananas

- 1/2 cup natural peanut butter

- 2 cups whole wheat flour

- 1 teaspoon baking powder

Instructions:

1. In a bowl, mix mashed bananas and peanut butter until well combined.

2. Gradually add whole wheat flour and baking powder to the banana mixture, stirring until a dough forms.

3. Roll out the dough on a floured surface to about 1/4-inch thickness.

4. Use cookie cutters to cut out biscuit shapes.

5. Place the biscuits on a greased slow cooker insert.

6. Cover and cook on low for 3 hours or until biscuits are firm and golden brown.

7. Allow to cool before serving.

Nutritional Information: Protein: 5g, Fat: 8g, Carbohydrates: 20g, Fiber: 3g

Apple and Carrot Pupcakes

Servings: 12 pupcakes Cooking Time: 3 hours on low

Ingredients:

- 1 cup grated apples

- 1 cup grated carrots

- 2 cups whole wheat flour

- 2 eggs

- 1 teaspoon baking powder

Instructions:

1. In a bowl, mix grated apples, grated carrots, eggs, whole wheat flour, and baking powder until well combined.

2. Grease muffin cups or use paper liners in a muffin tin.

3. Spoon the batter evenly into the muffin cups.

4. Place the muffin tin in the slow cooker.

5. Cover and cook on low for 3 hours or until pupcakes are set and a toothpick inserted into the center comes out clean.

6. Allow to cool before serving.

Nutritional Information: Protein: 3g, Fat: 2g, Carbohydrates: 8g, Fiber: 1g

Chicken and Sweet Potato Jerky

Servings: Varies Cooking Time: 4 hours on low

Ingredients:

- 1 lb boneless, skinless chicken breasts

- 2 cups diced sweet potatoes

Instructions:

1. Slice the chicken breasts into thin strips.

2. Place the chicken strips and diced sweet potatoes in the slow cooker.

3. Cover and cook on low for 4 hours or until the chicken is fully cooked and the sweet potatoes are tender.

4. Remove from the slow cooker and allow to cool completely.

5. Slice the cooked chicken into bite-sized pieces.

6. Store in an airtight container in the refrigerator.

Nutritional Information: Protein: 22g, Fat: 2g, Carbohydrates: 16g, Fiber: 2g

Pumpkin and Oatmeal Cookies

Servings: Varies Cooking Time: 3 hours on low

Ingredients:

- 1 cup canned pumpkin puree

- 2 cups rolled oats

- 1/2 cup unsweetened applesauce

- 1 teaspoon ground cinnamon

Instructions:

1. In a bowl, mix pumpkin puree, rolled oats, applesauce, and ground cinnamon until well combined.

2. Drop spoonfuls of the mixture onto a greased slow cooker insert.

3. Flatten each cookie slightly with the back of a spoon.

4. Cover and cook on low for 3 hours or until cookies are firm and golden brown.

5. Allow to cool before serving.

Nutritional Information: Protein: 3g, Fat: 2g, Carbohydrates: 8g, Fiber: 1g

Turkey and Cranberry Meatballs

Servings: Varies Cooking Time: 4 hours on low

Ingredients:

- 1 lb ground turkey

- 1/2 cup dried cranberries, chopped

- 1 cup cooked quinoa

- 2 eggs

Instructions:

1. In a bowl, mix ground turkey, chopped dried cranberries, cooked quinoa, and eggs until well combined.

2. Shape the mixture into meatballs and place them in a single layer in the slow cooker insert.

3. Cover and cook on low for 4 hours or until meatballs are cooked through.

4. Allow to cool before serving.

Nutritional Information: Protein: 18g, Fat: 4g, Carbohydrates: 8g, Fiber: 1g

Beef and Carrot Doggy Loaf

Servings: Varies Cooking Time: 6 hours on low

Ingredients:

- 1 lb lean ground beef

- 2 cups grated carrots

- 1 cup rolled oats

- 2 eggs

Instructions:

1. In a bowl, mix ground beef, grated carrots, rolled oats, and eggs until well combined.

2. Shape the mixture into a loaf shape and place it in a greased slow cooker insert.

3. Cover and cook on low for 6 hours or until the loaf is cooked through.

4. Allow to cool before slicing and serving.

Nutritional Information: Protein: 20g, Fat: 10g, Carbohydrates: 16g, Fiber: 3g

Turkey and Pumpkin Pupcakes

Servings: 12 pup cakes Cooking Time: 3 hours on low

Ingredients:

- 1 cup canned pumpkin puree

- 1/2 cup plain yogurt

- 2 eggs

- 2 cups whole wheat flour

- 1 teaspoon baking powder

Instructions:

1. In a bowl, mix pumpkin puree, plain yogurt, and eggs until well combined.

2. Add whole wheat flour and baking powder to the pumpkin mixture, stirring until a batter forms.

3. Grease muffin cups or use paper liners in a muffin tin.

4. Spoon the batter evenly into the muffin cups.

5. Place the muffin tin in the slow cooker.

6. Cover and cook on low for 3 hours or until pup cakes are set and a toothpick inserted into the centre comes out clean.

7. Allow to cool before serving.

Nutritional Information: Protein: 3g, Fat: 2g, Carbohydrates: 8g, Fiber: 1g

Chicken and Cheese Biscuits

Servings: Varies Cooking Time: 3 hours on low

Ingredients:

- 1 cup cooked, shredded chicken

- 1/2 cup shredded cheddar cheese

- 1 cup whole wheat flour

- 1/4 cup unsweetened applesauce

Instructions:

1. In a bowl, mix shredded chicken, shredded cheddar cheese, whole wheat flour, and unsweetened applesauce until well combined.

2. Roll out the dough on a floured surface to about 1/4-inch thickness.

3. Use cookie cutters to cut out biscuit shapes.

4. Place the biscuits on a greased slow cooker insert.

5. Cover and cook on low for 3 hours or until biscuits are firm and golden brown.

6. Allow to cool before serving.

Nutritional Information: Protein: 5g, Fat: 8g, Carbohydrates: 20g, Fiber: 3g

Salmon and Sweet Potato Bites

Servings: Varies Cooking Time: 4 hours on low

Ingredients:

- 1 can (14 oz) salmon, drained and flaked

- 1 cup mashed sweet potatoes

- 1/2 cup almond flour

- 2 eggs

Instructions:

1. In a bowl, mix flaked salmon, mashed sweet potatoes, almond flour, and eggs until well combined.

2. Drop spoonfuls of the mixture onto a greased slow cooker insert.

3. Flatten each bite slightly with the back of a spoon.

4. Cover and cook on low for 4 hours or until bites are firm.

5. Allow to cool before serving.

Nutritional Information: Protein: 20g, Fat: 10g, Carbohydrates: 22g, Fiber: 5g

Turkey and Blueberry Muffins

Servings: 12 muffins Cooking Time: 3 hours on low

Ingredients:

- 1 cup cooked, shredded turkey

- 1/2 cup blueberries

- 2 cups whole wheat flour

- 1 teaspoon baking powder

- 2 eggs

Instructions:

1. In a bowl, mix shredded turkey, blueberries, whole wheat flour, baking powder, and eggs until well combined.

2. Grease muffin cups or use paper liners in a muffin tin.

3. Spoon the batter evenly into the muffin cups.

4. Place the muffin tin in the slow cooker.

5. Cover and cook on low for 3 hours or until muffins are set and a toothpick inserted into the center comes out clean.

6. Allow to cool before serving.

Nutritional Information: Protein: 3g, Fat: 2g, Carbohydrates: 8g, Fiber: 1g

CHAPTER 8
Special Dietary Considerations Dogs with Specific Needs

Grain-Free Chicken and Vegetable Stew

Servings: 4 Cooking Time: 4 hours on low

Ingredients:

- 1 lb boneless, skinless chicken thighs, diced
- 1 cup diced sweet potatoes
- 1 cup chopped green beans
- 1 cup diced zucchini
- 4 cups low-sodium chicken broth

Instructions:

1. Place diced chicken thighs, sweet potatoes, green beans, and zucchini in the slow cooker.
2. Pour low-sodium chicken broth over the ingredients.
3. Cover and cook on low for 4 hours or until chicken is cooked through and vegetables are tender.
4. Stir well before serving.

Nutritional Information: Protein: 24g, Fat: 10g, Carbohydrates: 20g, Fiber: 4g

Low-Fat Turkey and Rice Casserole

Servings: 6 Cooking Time: 4 hours on low

Ingredients:

- 1 lb ground turkey breast

- 1 cup cooked brown rice

- 2 cups chopped carrots

- 1 cup chopped spinach

- 4 cups low-sodium turkey or chicken broth

Instructions:

1. In a skillet, cook ground turkey breast until browned. Drain excess fat.

2. Place cooked ground turkey in the slow cooker.

3. Add cooked brown rice, chopped carrots, chopped spinach, and low-sodium broth to the slow cooker.

4. Cover and cook on low for 4 hours or until carrots are tender.

5. Stir well before serving.

Nutritional Information: Protein: 18g, Fat: 2g, Carbohydrates: 16g, Fiber: 4g

Sensitive Stomach Lamb and Potato Stew

Servings: 4 Cooking Time: 6 hours on low

Ingredients:

- 1 lb lean lamb stew meat, cubed

- 2 cups diced potatoes

- 1 cup chopped carrots

- 1 cup chopped green beans

- 4 cups low-sodium lamb or beef broth

Instructions:

1. Place cubed lamb stew meat, diced potatoes, chopped carrots, and chopped green beans in the slow cooker.

2. Pour low-sodium lamb or beef broth over the ingredients.

3. Cover and cook on low for 6 hours or until lamb is tender and vegetables are cooked through.

4. Stir well before serving.

Nutritional Information: Protein: 22g, Fat: 8g, Carbohydrates: 18g, Fiber: 5g

Weight Management Turkey and Pumpkin Stew

Servings: 4 Cooking Time: 4 hours on low

Ingredients:

- 1 lb ground turkey

- 1 cup canned pumpkin puree

- 2 cups chopped green beans

- 1 cup chopped carrots

- 4 cups low-sodium turkey or chicken broth

Instructions:

1. In a skillet, cook ground turkey until browned. Drain excess fat.

2. Place cooked ground turkey in the slow cooker.

3. Add canned pumpkin puree, chopped green beans, chopped carrots, and low-sodium broth to the slow cooker.

4. Cover and cook on low for 4 hours or until vegetables are tender.

5. Stir well before serving.

Nutritional Information: Protein: 22g, Fat: 8g, Carbohydrates: 18g, Fiber: 5g

Joint Health Chicken and Glucosamine Stew

Servings: 4 Cooking Time: 4 hours on low

Ingredients:

- 1 lb boneless, skinless chicken thighs, diced

- 2 cups chopped sweet potatoes

- 1 cup chopped carrots

- 1 cup chopped celery

- 4 cups low-sodium chicken broth

- 1 tablespoon glucosamine powder

Instructions:

1. Place diced chicken thighs, chopped sweet potatoes, chopped carrots, and chopped celery in the slow cooker.

2. Dissolve glucosamine powder in low-sodium chicken broth, then pour over the ingredients in the slow cooker.

3. Cover and cook on low for 4 hours or until chicken is cooked through and vegetables are tender.

4. Stir well before serving.

Nutritional Information: Protein: 24g, Fat: 10g, Carbohydrates: 20g, Fiber: 4g

Digestive Health Beef and Pumpkin Stew

Servings: 4 Cooking Time: 6 hours on low

Ingredients:

- 1 lb lean beef stew meat, cubed

- 2 cups diced pumpkin

- 1 cup chopped green beans

- 1 cup chopped carrots

- 4 cups low-sodium beef broth

- 1/4 cup plain yogurt (added after cooking)

Instructions:

1. Place cubed beef stew meat, diced pumpkin, chopped green beans, and chopped carrots in the slow cooker.

2. Pour low-sodium beef broth over the ingredients.

3. Cover and cook on low for 6 hours or until beef is tender and vegetables are cooked through.

4. Stir in plain yogurt just before serving.

5. Stir well before serving.

Nutritional Information: Protein: 24g, Fat: 10g, Carbohydrates: 20g, Fiber: 4g

Allergen-Free Turkey and Rice Casserole

Servings: 6 Cooking Time: 4 hours on low

Ingredients:

- 1 lb ground turkey breast

- 2 cups cooked white rice

- 1 cup diced carrots

- 1 cup diced zucchini

- 4 cups low-sodium turkey or chicken broth

Instructions:

1. In a skillet, cook ground turkey breast until browned. Drain excess fat.

2. Place cooked ground turkey in the slow cooker.

3. Add cooked white rice, diced carrots, diced zucchini, and low-sodium broth to the slow cooker.

4. Cover and cook on low for 4 hours or until vegetables are tender.

5. Stir well before serving.

Nutritional Information: Protein: 18g, Fat: 2g, Carbohydrates: 16g, Fiber: 4g

Low-Calorie Chicken and Vegetable Soup

Servings: 4 Cooking Time: 4 hours on low

Ingredients:

- 1 lb boneless, skinless chicken breasts

- 2 cups chopped broccoli

- 1 cup chopped cauliflower

- 1 cup chopped bell peppers

- 4 cups low-sodium chicken broth

Instructions:

1. Place chicken breasts, chopped broccoli, chopped cauliflower, and chopped bell peppers in the slow cooker.

2. Pour low-sodium chicken broth over the ingredients.

3. Cover and cook on low for 4 hours or until chicken is cooked through and vegetables are tender.

4. Shred the chicken using forks before serving.

5. Stir well before serving.

Nutritional Information: Protein: 24g, Fat: 10g, Carbohydrates: 20g, Fiber: 4g

Senior Dog Turkey and Rice Stew

Servings: 4 Cooking Time: 6 hours on low

Ingredients:

- 1 lb ground turkey

- 2 cups cooked brown rice

- 1 cup chopped carrots

- 1 cup chopped green beans

- 4 cups low-sodium turkey or chicken broth

Instructions:

1. In a skillet, cook ground turkey until browned. Drain excess fat.

2. Place cooked ground turkey in the slow cooker.

3. Add cooked brown rice, chopped carrots, chopped green beans, and low-sodium broth to the slow cooker.

4. Cover and cook on low for 6 hours or until vegetables are tender.

5. Stir well before serving.

Nutritional Information: Protein: 18g, Fat: 2g, Carbohydrates: 16g, Fiber: 4g

Low-Protein Beef and Barley Stew

Servings: 4 Cooking Time: 6 hours on low

Ingredients:

- 1 lb lean beef stew meat, cubed

- 2 cups cooked barley

- 1 cup chopped carrots

- 1 cup chopped celery

- 4 cups low-sodium beef broth

Instructions:

1. Place cubed beef stew meat, cooked barley, chopped carrots, and chopped celery in the slow cooker.

2. Pour low-sodium beef broth over the ingredients.

3. Cover and cook on low for 6 hours or until beef is tender and vegetables are cooked through.

4. Stir well before serving.

Nutritional Information: Protein: 22g, Fat: 8g, Carbohydrates: 18g, Fiber: 5g

CONCLUSION

As I reflect on the pages of this cookbook, I am filled with a profound sense of fulfillment and purpose. What began as a journey born out of love for a single Beagle named Dan has evolved into a lifelong commitment to the health and well-being of Beagles everywhere.

Throughout these recipes, I've poured my heart and soul into creating meals that not only nourish the bodies of our furry companions but also ignite their spirits and bring joy to their lives. Each dish is a labor of love, crafted with care and attention to detail to ensure that every bite is packed with the essential nutrients Beagles need to thrive.

But this cookbook is more than just a collection of recipes; it's a testament to the power of love, dedication, and the transformative impact of wholesome nutrition. It's a celebration of the bond between Beagles and their human companions, and a reminder of the profound responsibility we have to care for these beloved creatures.

As I turn the final page of this cookbook, I am reminded of the countless Beagles whose lives have been touched by the power of good nutrition. From Dan, whose journey inspired this book, to the countless patients I've had the privilege of caring for over the years, each story serves as a testament to the incredible difference that proper nutrition can make.

But my journey doesn't end here. As I continue to explore the world of canine nutrition, I invite you to join me. Your feedback and honest reviews are invaluable as I strive to improve and innovate, ensuring that this cookbook remains a trusted resource for Beagle parents for generations to come.

So please, take a moment to share your thoughts and experiences with me. Whether you found a particular recipe to be a hit with your furry friend or have suggestions for improvement, I welcome your feedback with open arms.

Together, let's continue to nourish our Beagles with love, care, and the power of wholesome nutrition. Thank you for embarking on this journey with me, and may your tails wag with joy and your hearts be filled with love.

BONUS 1
Fun Activities for Beagles

Beagles are known for their boundless energy, curious nature, and keen sense of smell. Keeping them mentally and physically stimulated is essential for their overall well-being and happiness. In this chapter, we'll explore a variety of fun activities tailored to the energetic and playful nature of beagles. From outdoor adventures to interactive games, these activities will provide enrichment and enjoyment for your furry friend.

1. Scent Tracking: Beagles have an exceptional sense of smell, making scent tracking an ideal activity to engage their natural instincts. Set up a scent trail using treats or toys in your backyard or a nearby park. Start with simple trails and gradually increase the difficulty as your beagle becomes more adept at tracking. This activity not only provides mental stimulation but also reinforces obedience and focus.

2. Hide and Seek: Hide and seek is a classic game that beagles love. Have a family member or friend hold your beagle's attention while you hide in another room or behind furniture. Then, call out your beagle's name and encourage them to find you. Use treats or a Favorite toy as a reward when they successfully locate you. This game not only builds a strong bond between you and your beagle but also sharpens their problem-solving skills.

3. Interactive Puzzle Toys: Interactive puzzle toys are excellent for keeping beagles mentally stimulated and entertained. Invest in a variety of puzzle toys that challenge your beagle to use their problem-solving skills to access treats or food hidden inside. These toys can range from simple treat-

dispensing balls to more complex puzzles that require pushing, pulling, or rotating mechanisms.

4. Agility Training: Agility training is a fantastic way to channel your beagle's energy into a constructive and fun activity. Set up a makeshift agility course in your backyard using everyday household items like cones, tunnels, hurdles, and ramps. Teach your beagle to navigate the course, weaving through obstacles, jumping over hurdles, and crawling through tunnels. Agility training not only provides physical exercise but also strengthens the bond between you and your beagle through positive reinforcement.

5. Fetch and Retrieve: Beagles love to chase and retrieve objects, making fetch a classic game for this breed. Use a ball, Frisbee, or plush toy and throw it a short distance for your beagle to retrieve. Start with short throws and gradually increase the distance as your beagle becomes more proficient. Incorporate obedience commands like "fetch" and "drop it" to reinforce training while playing. Remember to use soft toys to protect your beagle's teeth and prevent injury.

6. Swimming: Many beagles enjoy swimming and splashing around in water, making it an excellent activity, especially during the hot summer months. If you have access to a safe swimming area like a pool, lake, or beach, introduce your beagle to the water gradually and ensure they feel comfortable before encouraging them to swim. Always supervise your beagle while swimming and provide flotation devices if needed, especially for novice swimmers.

7. Treks and Hikes: Beagles thrive on outdoor adventures and love exploring new environments. Take your beagle on treks and hikes through parks, trails, or nature reserves where they can sniff and explore to their heart's

content. Be mindful of your beagle's energy levels and physical capabilities and bring plenty of water and snacks for breaks along the way. Remember to keep your beagle on a leash or harness to ensure their safety and prevent them from wandering off.

BONUS 2
30 Day Meal Plan

Day	Breakfast	Lunch	Dinner	Snacks
1	Peanut Butter and Banana Biscuits	Turkey and Sweet Potato Stew	Chicken and Vegetable Casserole	Carrot Sticks
2	Apple and Carrot Pupcakes	Beef and Barley Soup	Salmon and Sweet Potato Bites	Blueberries
3	Pumpkin and Oatmeal Cookies	Chicken and Rice Casserole	Turkey and Pumpkin Stew	Green Beans
4	Turkey and Cranberry Meatballs	Lentil and Vegetable Stew	Beef and Vegetable Stir-Fry	Plain Yogurt
5	Salmon and Spinach Risotto	Chicken and Quinoa Salad	Turkey and Green Bean Casserole	Apple Slices
6	Chicken and Cheese Biscuits	Beef and Potato Stew	Turkey and Carrot Casserole	Frozen Peas
7	Beef and Carrot Doggy Loaf	Turkey and Brown Rice Soup	Chicken and Broccoli Casserole	Watermelon

8	Turkey and Blueberry Muffins	Chicken and Sweet Potato Chili	Beef and Vegetable Stew	Cooked Pumpkin
9	Sweet Potato and Chicken Hash	Turkey and Lentil Soup	Salmon and Spinach Risotto	Celery Sticks
10	Pumpkin and Peanut Butter Bites	Beef and Kale Stew	Chicken and Rice Casserole	Frozen Blueberries
11	Turkey and Cranberry Meatballs	Lentil and Vegetable Curry	Turkey and Green Bean Casserole	Sliced Cucumber
12	Chicken and Cheese Biscuits	Beef and Sweet Potato Chili	Salmon and Sweet Potato Bites	Baby Carrots
13	Turkey and Blueberry Muffins	Chicken and Quinoa Salad	Beef and Vegetable Stir-Fry	Sliced Apples
14	Peanut Butter and Banana Biscuits	Turkey and Brown Rice Soup	Chicken and Broccoli Casserole	Frozen Green Beans
15	Apple and Carrot Pupcakes	Lentil and Vegetable Stew	Beef and Potato Stew	Plain Rice Cakes
16	Pumpkin and Oatmeal Cookies	Chicken and Sweet Potato Stew	Turkey and Carrot Casserole	Cooked Broccoli

17	Salmon and Spinach Risotto	Beef and Barley Soup	Turkey and Green Bean Casserole	Frozen Strawberries
18	Chicken and Cheese Biscuits	Turkey and Lentil Soup	Beef and Vegetable Stew	Sliced Bell Peppers
19	Turkey and Blueberry Muffins	Beef and Potato Stew	Salmon and Spinach Risotto	Cherry Tomatoes
20	Beef and Carrot Doggy Loaf	Chicken and Quinoa Salad	Chicken and Rice Casserole	Apple Slices
21	Sweet Potato and Chicken Hash	Lentil and Vegetable Curry	Turkey and Brown Rice Soup	Blueberries
22	Turkey and Cranberry Meatballs	Beef and Sweet Potato Chili	Chicken and Broccoli Casserole	Frozen Peas
23	Chicken and Cheese Biscuits	Turkey and Green Bean Casserole	Beef and Vegetable Stir-Fry	Carrot Sticks
24	Turkey and Blueberry Muffins	Chicken and Brown Rice Soup	Salmon and Sweet Potato Bites	Watermelon
25	Pumpkin and Peanut Butter Bites	Beef and Kale Stew	Turkey and Carrot Casserole	Sliced Cucumber

26	Peanut Butter and Banana Biscuits	Chicken and Quinoa Salad	Beef and Potato Stew	Frozen Blueberries
27	Apple and Carrot Pupcakes	Turkey and Lentil Soup	Chicken and Rice Casserole	Sliced Bell Peppers
28	Pumpkin and Oatmeal Cookies	Beef and Barley Soup	Turkey and Green Bean Casserole	Baby Carrots
29	Salmon and Spinach Risotto	Chicken and Sweet Potato Stew	Beef and Vegetable Stew	Frozen Green Beans
30	Chicken and Cheese Biscuits	Turkey and Brown Rice Soup	Chicken and Broccoli Casserole	Sliced Apples

WEEKLY —

Meal Planner

Week of:

Monday

BREAKFAST

LUNCH

DINNER

SNACK

Tuesday

BREAKFAST

LUNCH

DINNER

SNACK

Wednesday

BREAKFAST

LUNCH

DINNER

SNACK

Thursday

BREAKFAST

LUNCH

DINNER

SNACK

Friday

BREAKFAST

LUNCH

DINNER

SNACK

Saturday

BREAKFAST

LUNCH

DINNER

SNACK

Sunday

BREAKFAST

LUNCH

DINNER

SNACK

NOTES:

Meal Planner

Week of:

Monday	Tuesday	Wednesday
BREAKFAST	BREAKFAST	BREAKFAST
LUNCH	LUNCH	LUNCH
DINNER	DINNER	DINNER
SNACK	SNACK	SNACK

Thursday	Friday	Saturday
BREAKFAST	BREAKFAST	BREAKFAST
LUNCH	LUNCH	LUNCH
DINNER	DINNER	DINNER
SNACK	SNACK	SNACK

Sunday	NOTES:
BREAKFAST	
LUNCH	
DINNER	
SNACK	

Meal Planner

Week of:

Monday	Tuesday	Wednesday
BREAKFAST	BREAKFAST	BREAKFAST
LUNCH	LUNCH	LUNCH
DINNER	DINNER	DINNER
SNACK	SNACK	SNACK

Thursday	Friday	Saturday
BREAKFAST	BREAKFAST	BREAKFAST
LUNCH	LUNCH	LUNCH
DINNER	DINNER	DINNER
SNACK	SNACK	SNACK

Sunday	NOTES:
BREAKFAST	
LUNCH	
DINNER	
SNACK	

Meal Planner

Week of:

Monday	Tuesday	Wednesday
BREAKFAST	BREAKFAST	BREAKFAST
LUNCH	LUNCH	LUNCH
DINNER	DINNER	DINNER
SNACK	SNACK	SNACK

Thursday	Friday	Saturday
BREAKFAST	BREAKFAST	BREAKFAST
LUNCH	LUNCH	LUNCH
DINNER	DINNER	DINNER
SNACK	SNACK	SNACK

Sunday	NOTES:
BREAKFAST	
LUNCH	
DINNER	
SNACK	

Meal Planner

Week of:

Monday	Tuesday	Wednesday
BREAKFAST	BREAKFAST	BREAKFAST
LUNCH	LUNCH	LUNCH
DINNER	DINNER	DINNER
SNACK	SNACK	SNACK

Thursday	Friday	Saturday
BREAKFAST	BREAKFAST	BREAKFAST
LUNCH	LUNCH	LUNCH
DINNER	DINNER	DINNER
SNACK	SNACK	SNACK

Sunday	NOTES:
BREAKFAST	
LUNCH	
DINNER	
SNACK	

Meal Planner

Week of:

Monday			Tuesday			Wednesday
BREAKFAST			BREAKFAST			BREAKFAST
LUNCH			LUNCH			LUNCH
DINNER			DINNER			DINNER
SNACK			SNACK			SNACK

Thursday			Friday			Saturday
BREAKFAST			BREAKFAST			BREAKFAST
LUNCH			LUNCH			LUNCH
DINNER			DINNER			DINNER
SNACK			SNACK			SNACK

Sunday	NOTES:
BREAKFAST	
LUNCH	
DINNER	
SNACK	

Meal Planner

Week of:

Monday	**Tuesday**	**Wednesday**
BREAKFAST	BREAKFAST	BREAKFAST
LUNCH	LUNCH	LUNCH
DINNER	DINNER	DINNER
SNACK	SNACK	SNACK
Thursday	**Friday**	**Saturday**
BREAKFAST	BREAKFAST	BREAKFAST
LUNCH	LUNCH	LUNCH
DINNER	DINNER	DINNER
SNACK	SNACK	SNACK

Sunday	NOTES:
BREAKFAST	
LUNCH	
DINNER	
SNACK	

Meal Planner

Week of:

Monday	Tuesday	Wednesday
BREAKFAST	BREAKFAST	BREAKFAST
LUNCH	LUNCH	LUNCH
DINNER	DINNER	DINNER
SNACK	SNACK	SNACK

Thursday	Friday	Saturday
BREAKFAST	BREAKFAST	BREAKFAST
LUNCH	LUNCH	LUNCH
DINNER	DINNER	DINNER
SNACK	SNACK	SNACK

Sunday	NOTES:
BREAKFAST	
LUNCH	
DINNER	
SNACK	

Meal Planner

Week of:

Monday	Tuesday	Wednesday
BREAKFAST	BREAKFAST	BREAKFAST
LUNCH	LUNCH	LUNCH
DINNER	DINNER	DINNER
SNACK	SNACK	SNACK

Thursday	Friday	Saturday
BREAKFAST	BREAKFAST	BREAKFAST
LUNCH	LUNCH	LUNCH
DINNER	DINNER	DINNER
SNACK	SNACK	SNACK

Sunday	NOTES:
BREAKFAST	
LUNCH	
DINNER	
SNACK	

Meal Planner

Week of:

Monday		
BREAKFAST		
LUNCH		
DINNER		
SNACK		

Tuesday		
BREAKFAST		
LUNCH		
DINNER		
SNACK		

Wednesday		
BREAKFAST		
LUNCH		
DINNER		
SNACK		

Thursday		
BREAKFAST		
LUNCH		
DINNER		
SNACK		

Friday		
BREAKFAST		
LUNCH		
DINNER		
SNACK		

Saturday		
BREAKFAST		
LUNCH		
DINNER		
SNACK		

Sunday		
BREAKFAST		
LUNCH		
DINNER		
SNACK		

NOTES:

Meal Planner

Month of:

Sun	Mon	Tues	Wed	Thurs	Fri	Sai